FROM THE GROUND UP

Poems of One Southerner's
Passage to Adulthood

Books by
ROBERT HAMBLIN

Poetry

Perpendicular Rain (1986)

Bibliography (Coedited with Louis Daniel Brodsky)

Selections from the William Faulkner Collection of
  Louis Daniel Brodsky: A Descriptive Catalogue (1979)
Faulkner: A Comprehensive Guide to the Brodsky Collection
    Volume I: The Biobibliography (1982)
    Volume II: The Letters (1984)
    Volume III: The De Gaulle Story (1984)
    Volume IV: Battle Cry (1985)
    Volume V: Manuscripts and Documents (1989)
Country Lawyer and Other Stories for the Screen by William
    Faulkner (1987)
Stallion Road: A Screenplay by William Faulkner (1989)

Biography

Win or Win: A Season with Ron Shumate (1993)

FROM THE GROUND UP

Poems of One Southerner's
Passage to Adulthood

by Robert Hamblin

TIME BEING BOOKS
POETRY IN SIGHT AND SOUND
Saint Louis, Missouri

Time Being Books
10411 Clayton Road
Saint Louis, Missouri 63131

Time Being Books volumes are printed on acid-free paper, and binding
materials are chosen for strength and durability.

Library of Congress Catalog Card Number:

ISBN 1-877770-64-7
ISBN 1-877770-65-5 (pbk.)
ISBN 1-877770-67-1 (tape)

Book Designed by Ruth A. Dambach
Cover Designed by Kathryn McDaniel Smith
Southeast Missouri State University
Manufactured in the United States of America

First Edition, first printing (October 1992)

Acknowledgments

A number of the poems in this book first appeared in *The Cape Rock* and *The Ozark Review*. I am grateful to the editors of those journals for permission to reprint those poems. Some have been revised for inclusion here.

I am pleased to acknowledge a particular indebtedness to a group of special friends and colleagues — my fellow editors of *The Cape Rock*. In my nearly twenty-five-year association with that journal, it has been my good fortune to work with a number of outstanding editors and poets. I am thinking especially of the succession of general editors — Peter Hilty, Max Cordonnier, Robert Burns, Ted Hirschfield, and Harvey Hecht — and associate editors John Bierk, Dale Haskell, Pamela Hearn, and Janice Rainwater. My life, as well as my poetry, has been immeasurably enriched through my friendship with these remarkable and dedicated individuals.

Over the years several other poets, editors, colleagues, and friends have responded to my poems with helpful advice and encouragement. I want to thank, particularly, Ann Abadie, Dorothy Abbott, Terry Begley, L.D. Brodsky, Charles Ghigna, Jack Higgs, John Hinni, Don Johnson, Jay Martin, Jim Nicholson, Lyle Olsen, John Owen, Alan Pater, John Pilkington, David Vanderwerken, and Gerald Walton.

By far my greatest debt, actually inexpressible, is acknowledged on the dedication page.

For Kaye,
my beloved wife

Contents

Part Three: World's Stage

Part Four: Darkness Rises

FROM THE GROUND UP

Poems of One Southerner's
Passage to Adulthood

I'd like to get away from earth awhile
And then come back to it and begin over.
May no fate willfully misunderstand me
And half grant what I wish and snatch me away
Not to return. Earth's the right place for love:
I don't know where it's likely to go better.

— Robert Frost, "Birches"

Part One:
TIMEPIECES

* This symbol is used to indicate that a stanza has been divided
because of pagination.

The Cannons

You get there by turning off Highway 45
at Baldwyn and following the county road,
now paved, west for six miles
until you reach the crossroads.
You'll know you're there when you see
the monument and the cannons.

The steel-wire fence is gone now,
and the decorative iron gates,
which were never locked but always
chained shut to keep the children out,
and the spirits in. Gone, too,
is the general store across the road,
my father's, with the rooms in back
in which I lived as a boy.

Historical markers now dot the wide
expanse of velveteen lawn,
documenting for northern tourists
and other visitors the battlefield maneuvers
of long-dead Union and Confederate soldiers.
Today, strangely, I am one of those
tourists, though for me the markers
are altogether redundant, adding nothing
to the indelible stories traced
on my memory by old men, my grandfather
among them, on this same ground years ago.

Still today, through a forced breach in time,
I see them sitting on the veranda
of the store in warm weather,
or, during winter, gathered inside
around the pot-bellied stove, repeating
the stories they had from their fathers,
about how, just down the road there,
where Brice's house then stood,
old "Fustest with the Mostest" Forrest
ambushed that "Damn Yankee" Sturgis
*

and sent him and what little survived
of his army hightailing it back
toward Ripley and Memphis.

Just a boy, I frequently sat
on that veranda watching Pappy Hickey
and the other old-timers whittle
or play checkers or dominoes and listening
as they recounted the story over and over.
Pappy said that his father, my great-grandfather,
a 14-year-old wagon driver for Forrest's cavalry,
hid under the floor of the Brice house
and watched the battle unfold. At the height
of the conflict a fatally-wounded Yankee,
seeking refuge under the same house,
died just a few yards from the spot
where my ancestor lay hidden.

Hearing these stories, I became,
for the only time in my life until now,
a serious historian, walking the beeswax
gullies after rains and searching
for exposed minieballs and grapeshot.
On one such walk I discovered
for the first time the small Confederate
burial ground in the pasture
just beyond the Presbyterian cemetery:
twelve graves in all, each marked
by a tiny marble stone, weather-stained,
all but one showing the inhabitant
of the grave as "Unknown." Even then
I regretted that of the hundreds of soldiers
who were killed in the battle, only twelve
were given graves, and only one of those
buried with his name: "Hardin Gilbert
Died June 10, 1864 19 Y'rs 8 Mo's 23 Da's."

Today, returning to this place in middle age,
I walk the grounds, read again the history
lesson carved into stone, try to resurrect
the contours of childhood and youth,
observe how the surrounding landscape,
like so much of life, steadily falls away
from this sharply-remembered scene.
I rub my hand over the cold steel of the cannon
and, surely not for the first time in my life,
though I do not recall doing it before,
whimsically take sight down the barrel to see
where it is aimed. I am shocked
to see that it is directed toward the empty lot
where my father's store once stood.
While I've been away some unknown phantom,
perhaps the ghost of one of the dead soldiers,
has loaded the weapon and fired it
at my childhood home, blowing it clean away.

The monument is still here, and the cannons,
but the only thing remaining across the road
is the chinaberry tree that stood beside
our kitchen window and cast, on sunny days,
insubstantial shadows that crept, relentless
as time, across the linoleum floor to the table
at which my mother, every morning after breakfast,
sat reading her Bible and praying.

Farm Mother

Most Saturdays, just a boy,
he accompanied her into the backyard
and even helped entice the hens
and pullets into easy plucking distance,
watching her clutch the bucketed apron
in one hand and with the other
broadcast the grains of corn
or the leftover cornbread crumbs
about her feet, matter-of-factly waiting
for the everlasting hunger to displace,
as it always, inevitably did,
the instinctive, nervous caution
and bring the family's Sunday dinner
within arm's reach.

"Chick, chick, chick," he mimicked
his mother, kneeling in overalls
on the hard, stubborn ground,
holding his supple cat's body in check
while she said, "Not that one, not that one,"
then, on command, grabbing "That one!"
in both hands, squeezing for dear life
the frail, trembling body
as he braced his ears against the loud,
frantic squawking and turned his face
from the terror of the fanning wings
while the remainder of the flock raced
or flew for cover under the house
or into the chinaberry tree.

Each time he felt himself falling
into a spinning void, but each time
he would be rescued by his mother's hand.
Grasping the hen firmly by the neck,
she would wring it round and round
as she did the windlass on the well,
*

or as his father whipped the crank
on the Ford tractor, then toss
its broken body to the ground.
Mother and son together watched
the final, futile dance of death:
the broken neck flopping like a string,
legs wobbling drunkenly, wings and body
thrashing about like a fish jerked
from water and thrown onto a creek bank.

On Sunday mornings, dressed
in his best shirt and pants and only tie,
he sat stiffly between his mother
and father on a wooden pew
in a crossroads primitive Baptist church
and sometimes even listened
as the preacher spoke of sin and death
and damnation and Jesus' sacrifice
on the cross. Older, though washed
in the faith and baptized into belief,
he could never rightly divide
the notions of love and salvation
and peace as he ate the flesh
and drank the blood. Like Sunday
dinner with chicken on the table
and the preacher as a house guest.

Winter nights, even after
he was much too old to do so,
and against his father's wishes,
he was sometimes allowed to crawl
into bed with his parents, curling
between them into the feathery down,
drawing his body heat from theirs,
seeking courage in their sure, steady
heartbeats and slow, rhythmic breathing.
*

Often, just before sleep
bore him away, he would reach
his hand to his mother's breast,
cupping her nipple in his fragile palm.
Even in the dark he saw her flesh
grow white as a plucked chicken's breast,
and prayed for his trembling heart
to lie silent and still.

Projectionist

Once a week he climbed the balcony stairs
of the Lyric Theater in Baldwyn to the upper room
where his Uncle Alfred threaded the projector with reel
after reel of Saturday matinee westerns.

He sat on a metal stool and traced down a silver shaft
of light the stagecoach adventures of a multitude
of heroes: Roy Rogers, Gene Autry, Hopalong Cassidy,
Lash LaRue, the Durango Kid, Johnny Mack Brown.

Whatever the image on the screen, the world at that stage
of life was always black and white, villains as obvious
as the beards and black hats and nondescript clothes
they wore. The good guys sang to their horses.

Later, after the onset of puberty, his world turned
technicolor with desire. Now he leered through peepholes
as Gable and Holden and Grant wooed and wowed Marilyn,
Kim, Sophia. Trigger and Champion were quickly forgotten.

Still he knew there was more. How much more he learned
the day he climbed the steps and discovered his uncle
with Mary Lou, the waitress at Clyde's Cafe, naked, riding
very high in the saddle. Dale Evans never rode like that.

After that he was invited to stay for the late, late show.
When the regular features had ended, Uncle Alfred previewed
for him the bumps, grinds, and other moves of Lily St. Cyr.
Thereafter he spent a lot of time at Clyde's Cafe.

Pre-Freudian

Years later, sitting in a huge
lecture hall on a Gothic, ivy-covered campus
in an eastern city, listening
to a bearded professor drone on and on
about Freud's and Jung's theories
of the human psyche, he immediately,
vividly remembered Tommy Ray Heard:

Who, when they were boys,
was always only too glad to volunteer
to rid the neighbors of any and all of their
unwanted cats. Once he accompanied him
on his mission, and watched
with shrinking breath as Tommy Ray,
brave beyond belief, stuffed
five stray kittens into a towsack,
tied the top with baling wire, gave the sack
a shake to get the cats acquainted,
then casually tossed the bundle
onto the ground and stood back
for the carnival to begin.

Again he sees the towsack thrashing
about his feet like a huge, hurt bird,
hears the squalling kittens
as they scratch and fight to escape the dark.
Then, the cats exhausted, or dead,
the towsack quiet as a mended mind
after torment, he watches the spreading patches
of blood seeping through the burlap bag,
frightening crimson flowers blossoming bright
as his mother's roses in the summer sun.

Later he follows Tommy Ray to the river
that runs behind the house, where together
they lift and toss their burden
as far as they can into the deepest water.
Whatever it is that remains in the dark,
*

silent womb of regret now sinks
slowly out of sight as small traces of blood
briefly appear, then disappear,
in the slow-moving current. But that night
he awoke in a cold sweat, frantic to catch
the spilled blood in the palms of his hands
and feeling the rigid stare of a cat's eyes
from the far corner of the ceiling.

Now the professor, finished with Freud,
has moved on to Jung. He listens
with the surface edge of thought
while his other self holds his breath
and dives down, down, down, in search
of marriage with his dark, lost brother.

Annie's Gold

To A.M.H.
Born December 15, 1892
Died ? ? ?

"There'll be gold
hanging off the trees
when you see me again,"
you told your family (now mine)
before you boarded the train
at the depot in Guntown, Mississippi,
on some lost day during the 1920's,
and disappeared forever.

A generation later, as children,
at family reunions or Christmas gatherings,
we learned that though you had gone away,
you would never really be allowed to leave us.
So we strained to grasp the words
as older relatives repeated your story,
or as much of it as they knew,
in hushed voices as far beyond us
as puberty, leaving us in our innocence
to imagine, in those wild, drowsy moments
before we drifted off to sleep,
what it might be like to wake
next morning and see all the limbs
of every tree dripping with gold.

Growing older, year by year,
our lives as nondescript and ordinary
as cotton slowly coming of age
on the parched hillside acres,
we patched together a crazy quilt
of your fabulous history:
your slender body and flaming red hair,
the train ticket you purchased to Birmingham,
the suspicions of an unhappy love affair,
*

even the rumored scandal of pregnancy,
talk of a quarrel with your brothers,
and their failure, a year later,
to trace your whereabouts, such failure
ending in speculation about your name change.

Now free to make of you what we would,
by turn our fantasizing saw you happy or forlorn,
wealthy or destitute, alive or dead.
But still we hoped, and half-believed,
that someday you might yet return.
At that stage we clung to a faith in metaphor,
finding in the first golden leaves of autumn
the sign you left to presage your coming.
But you were faithful to your vow to the end.
Another generation passed, and another,
and we repeated your story to our own children,
and they to theirs. Now mythic, you fired
their dreaming as you had ours: beautiful,
lost Annie, independent, passionate, mysterious,
as fiercely necessary to our mundane lives as God.

Now, four generations and seventy years
later, we all know you're never coming back:
yet you're still here with us,
locked in our collective memory
like a recessive gene. We still tell
your story to our children and grandchildren.
Every time a red-headed child is born
into the family someone will always remember
that Aunt Annie had bright red hair;
and every autumn, when maple and sassafras
lift their bright yellow skirts
and dance, defiantly, across the yard,
we say, hopefully, to ourselves
and to each other, "That's Annie's gold
hanging from the trees."

For Lizzie M—

An old letter, rusting,
fractured by time, discovered
by a curious, barefooted
boy in an old, unpainted,
abandoned Mississippi farmhouse:
from "Lizzie M—" to "Mr. S,"
a "Dear Friend," dated Cuthbert, Ga.,
December 20, 1894.

I hold the letter now,
almost a century later, in my hands,
in Cape Girardeau, Missouri,
its broken creases and fading ink
curling brooding thoughts
about my fingers like whispers,
telling of Bettie, the smart little girl
who enjoys reading Lizzie's letters,
and John Spence, who says he's
moving on to Texas as soon as possible,
and Noel, who "looks delicate
like a girl," of Mrs. Holman,
whose house sold too cheaply,
and "crazy old Mr. Byron," who peddles
God's judgment about the country,
and Charlie, who needs the address
of a fur dealer in St. Louis,
and Mildred, "refined nice and pretty,"
who intends going to Washington
even if she has to go by herself.

And this: "I will be surprised
if both of the Magnolias live."

Who were these people,
lost to history as to me,
and why do they appear
so significant now, heroic
even in their triteness?
*

And why have I, no kin
as my anonymous bequeather
undoubtedly was, kept
the letter these many years?

And why, here in midlife,
at the end of a different century,
do I so desperately hope
that the magnolias lived, and live,
and Mildred found her way
to Washington?

An Old Photograph

In fading daguerreotype
a farmhouse, unpeopled,
alien, afar.

Mind penetrates matter,
searches for a room,
a name, a face.

Identity escapes.

The house remains
an old photograph.

Never Dreaming, Then, of London

A young boy, no more than ten or eleven,
barefoot, since it is summer, and dressed
in bib overalls, sits on the front veranda
of a country crossroads general store.
He awaits the arrival of a crew of road hands,
who daily break from paving the gravel road
to purchase their lunch of potted meat and bologna
and crackers and R.C. Colas from his father.
All summer long, while the asphalt road magically
unwinds its spool of black ribbon toward town,
the boy listens to the raucous conversation
and laughter of the road gang: bold, virile
man-talk that both shames and exhilarates
his timid, yearning, uneventful years. One
of the workers carries a pack of Camels rolled up
in the sleeve of his tar-stained T-shirt
and wears a tatoo of the American eagle
on his upper arm. He recounts his experiences
Up North, where he worked for a time
in an automobile factory in Kenosha.
The boy hangs, excitedly, on every word.
At night, lying awake on the sweat-soaked sheet,
the only light the radio dial beside his bed,
he tunes his dreams to distant voices and music
from WCKY Cincinnati, KDKA Pittsburgh, WGN Chicago.
Years later, a man, and having seen those cities,
and more, the boy would still recall that summer
as the time when the road to town was paved.

Requital

Old man.
I watch you straddle
the barbed fence,
ache yourself over,
limp through bitterweeds
and piles of manure
to the pond below.

I follow,
wrestling with fishing rods
and tackle box,
dutiful son
if no longer a child,
fitting my path once more
to the diminishing measure
of your step.

We are different now,
you see that as well as I.
Still, each year we return
to this place to enact
the ancient ritual.

Today, though,
I leave the fishing to you;
I have other game to catch.
Careless of the lure
bouncing quietly on the water,
I watch you across the narrow lake
and recall how once there was
between us more than water,
a gulf too wide for casting.

But that was long ago:
today I sit idly
and trace my sinking youth
in the wrinkled absolution
of your face, grateful
for the armistice of age,
*

the peace that somehow survives
the rage of passion and regret.

Like that bass there,
which you now lead thrashing
across the violent wave
and lift with still strong
and steady hands into
the splendid, sun-splashed air.

View from Room 170

Past this antiseptic bed
on which my father wheezes
and groans toward death

Past the window
through which sunlight bleeds
the last drop of day

Past the excavated lot
where blackbirds stitch
at weeping wounds

Past the highway
where traffic drips like glucose
from a darkening tunnel

In an open field
with ash-gray ravines
nursed by scrawny trees

Wasted pieces of black tarpaper
lift and fall, flutter and fall
in an empty wind.

Mississippi Autumn

A harvest moon
climbs, with dreaming,
from orange to white
in the eastern sky.

Far below, trapped
on a narrow country road
behind wagon after wagon
loaded with cotton,
I long to push
the pedal to the floor,
break from the pack,
launch off from the nearest hill,
exiting this dry, dusty land
for a rendezvous
beyond the farthest star.

The Mantel Clock

"Your clock needs winding,"
she says, with none of the whimsical humor
she uses when she says, "Your dog wants out"
or "You need to talk to your son."

It *is* my clock, not hers,
like the dining room furniture and the piano,
legacies from her side of the family,
and not ours, like the pets and the children
and this house.

My father gave it to me, just weeks
before he died; he had it from his father,
who walked three miles to purchase it
at a Mississippi crossroads general store
on his wedding day in 1885.

I never knew those grandparents,
except through family stories repeated
for children on front verandas on hot
summer evenings while hundreds of mindless
fireflies mocked the darkness with their bright,
ephemeral flaming; and the old daguerreotype
now hanging in the upstairs hall:
the woman with the sad Indian features
and Irish name, the man, a hill farmer,
rigid in the unfamiliar suit, with mustache,
hawk-like nose, and cold, piercing eyes,
just the kind of man, perhaps, who would
purchase a clock on his wedding day.
They sit among six children, equally solemn.
The cherub on the front row is my father,
a lifetime removed from the cancer-ravaged
ghost I remember at the end.

Today it sits on the piano
in our living room in Cape Girardeau,
Missouri, wired securely to the wall
for protection against the impending
*

New Madrid earthquake. Its dark
mahogany cabinet is slightly streaked
and faded from its years on the mantel
above the butane heater in one of my several
childhood homes. Occasionally I think
I ought to have it refinished, but I never do.
The same for the broken matchstick,
a makeshift repair job by my father,
which still holds the circling hands in place.

For more than a century now,
its faithful pendulum swing and solid tick
have measured each half-second: 120 times
each minute, 172,800 each day,
more than sixty million times every year.
From any corner of the house, if we listen,
we can hear its striking every hour
and half-hour, the heavy downbeat marking
our steady progression through middle age
and on to whatever lies beyond.

Once a week, as regular as the sabbath,
I rewind it with the same original brass
key that my father used, and his father
before him, as will my son and grandson
after me. In those moments, epiphanies,
tuned to the intricate sounds of invisible gears
letting go of the past and storing up
the hours to come, I wait for the metronomic
rhythm to resume, reverberating through my mind
and body, stirring memory and desire,
seeking some depth of soul, rooting me in time,
this place, this house, this family.
Sometimes in such moments I imagine
the grandfather I never knew
standing beside me. Once, even,
he appeared to be smiling.

Part Two:
ANY SURPRISE OF LOVE

Riding Westward, 1983

Once,
in another country,
I traveled
a golden highway.

The sun,
in curious afterthought
to cloud and shower,
tilted a chalice
beyond a distant hill
and slid its surplus splendor
down a narrow sluice
of pavement,
becoming, for an instant,
one with earth.

It seemed
I could follow
that happy road
right into eternity.

Then heaven withdrew.
We drove on, into darkness.

Where the road led,
or what I was doing there,
I do not recall,
if I ever learned.

I remember only
a woman sat beside me,
and the gold, such gold.

Travelers

"I'm just another traveler on the road to Kingdom Come."
— *Harry Chapin*

In motel restaurants
I see them,
solitary as poets,
sipping their loneliness
like wine, dancing
their wills on the bold
incontinence of lounge music,
floating desire to distant rooms
where deep-mouthed waitresses
open their legs, joyfully,
to the mother-womb
of all returnings.

Newspaper in hand,
homeless as an unclaimed tip,
they walk the dull corridor,
turn the key,
bury their tameless eyes
in single, silent beds.

And always, when I see them,
I think of you, and feel
the visible touch of your
too, too invisible hands.

San Francisco, August 1977

> *"The key to the treasure is the treasure."*
> — *John Barth*

And now, the remembering:

After the cable cars
tumbled us, laughing,
up and down hills
to Chinatown and back,

After the minstrel crowds
on Fisherman's Wharf
mingled their merriment
with our love,

After the Golden Gate
funneled us, transformed,
beyond the city,
across the bay,

We walked, at dusk,
a mile to the shore
and watched the sun
go golden with the sea.

The waves,
in jubilation of our joy,
turned cartwheels
on the sand.

A Benediction

for Kaye

Do you remember
that night when, after màking love,
we lay quietly and listened
to the approaching storm?

Thunder splashed lightning
across the sky, blowing fear
past the inner edges of our souls.
Deep, untaught terror
chased the children to our door,
and together we sought the candled
safety of our basement room.

There, the children wrapped
in our too human arms,
we watched a violent wind
twist and thrash a climbing rosebush
against the window.

This was no earthly menace,
forcing entry, but something far more
definite and sinister.
How anything could endure such rage
we hardly knew.

Then we, and nature, slept.

The next morning we stood
among wasted leaves and petals
and marveled at a white rose,
perfect in bloom, graced
beyond the threatening night,
nestling in the shelter of the eaves.

Family Outing: At Giant City State Park

We leave the asphalt road
and climb a rocky path
through centuries.

Behind us the city,
patiently waiting to wrap us
again in familiar streets and voices,
knowing we could never betray ourselves
for long in this alien place.

We move slowly,
awkwardly,
like an aging athlete
whose muscles have forgotten
what the mind remembers,
or a blind man in a stranger's room.

The children seem more at home.
They race on ahead,
hopscotch on rocks
in the shallow stream,
pick mushrooms and wild flowers.
Their laughter stirs
strange memories
among murmuring echoes.

We picnic beneath a rock shelter,
its roof smoke-stained (so we've read)
from the campfires of primitive men.
We talk of these earlier occupants,
wonder of their notions of family,
survival, community, and love.

But Illinois is time, not place,
and we find nothing of ourselves
in conjecture of those ignorant even
of the bow and arrow
and the taming of the horse.

Still, I suppose,
one must be respectful:
I reclaim an empty beer can as we leave.

At the top of the hill
we hurriedly view the piled remains
of a stone fort, said to be
what's left of a giant buffalo trap,
hope for a food-filled paradise for early man.

The children, delighted,
climb among the ruins,
irreverently displacing rocks
that have lain quietly for ages.
At least they know the proper use of history,
not this indifferent respect.

Shortly, disappointed and bored,
we descend, anxious to be on the road
toward home. With us, uninvited
but real as the drizzle that cuts the skin,
go lingering thoughts
of a child's brittle laughter
and the earth's abiding stone.

For My Adopted Daughter

Stranger, daughter, friend:
the rivers of your past
come down to this odd emptying.

I have sought to trace
those rivers in your eyes,
deep subterranean passages
which brook no canoeing
but give back only my imaged self
buoyed in the grace of your presence.

Don't misunderstand;
it's no question of paternity
that leads me to search for origins
beneath the fondness of your bones,
but simply wonder, and gratitude,
for any surprise of love —
we two, in this strange place,
in this floating moment,
father and child,
reaching out with fragile hands
to scoop one shining pebble
from the darkening riverbed of time.

My Daughter at Her Guitar

Sounds from Laurie's guitar
skip through the house like a child
in ponytail, bringing delight
into my basement study.

I cease my own laboring
on an unfinished poem to listen
to your latest composition,
a happy tune that breaks the ice
from winter's longing, evokes dreams
of warm skies, bouncing water,
the green laughter of grass.

For three days now we have sought,
you in your upstairs room, I here,
to find in thought, word, sound
the elements of harmony,
to fashion from false starts,
dead ends, rearrangements, discord
a music to live by.

Sitting at my desk, pencil stayed,
I trace in your voice a resilience
I had almost forgotten I too possess.
Can it be just a week ago
you leaned, sobbing, into my arms
and asked questions no mere father
could answer, except with love,
that frail and silent prop we stand
against life's grim betrayal.
Still, it's all we have,
and, as you now remind me,
it is enough: today you sing,
and grace my heart with your song.

Children, make music for your fathers.
Sing them from their graves.
Bathe them in melody, unstop their ears,
liven their bones to know every sunrise
proves the earth reborn, and agony
is only the sound the heart makes
being tuned for joy.

Epiphany

Into the night,
in the privacy of my study,
I search for divinity
among my books.

Then you descend,
my little son,
shyly, pajama-clad,
sent by your mother's grace
to intrude a good night,
leaning your precious love
into my arms,
whispering God in the flesh.

For Steve, a United States Marine

I

It is 6:02 p.m., January 16, 1991.
Driving home from work, I have just heard
over the car radio that the world
has fallen apart, again. But this time
the event is very, very personal.
Driving on, tears welling in my eyes,
heart-stricken, I think of you and remember . . .

II

MCRD, San Diego, January 31, 1987, you,
guidon bearer for your platoon, marching
smartly at attention onto the parade ground,
your mother and I waiting proudly,
through binoculars, for you to grow big
as the beat of the bass drum,
recognizing your walk even at this huge distance,
despite its being reshaped and rigidly cast
into standard issue Marine Corps green.
Sitting in the grandstand with girlfriends,
wives, brothers, other parents, we watch
as you and your comrades circle the field
and pass in review. Ceremony over, now
a marine and no longer a recruit,
you collect a fifty-pushup wager
from the drill instructor you bested
in the last company run, then join us
for dinner at our hotel . . .

III

A summer day in Capaha Park, your first
bicycle solo at age seven, with me trotting along
beside to steady your start, anxiously guarding
your widening arcs stretching beyond my reach,
then racing to balance your fall
*

as you brake and leap beyond
the collapsing bike. Even then you were better
at moving out and on than stopping
or turning back. Already confident and cocky
as the dirt biker you will soon become,
you say you can do it yourself,
resent my interference, as also do the two
young lovers strolling nearby, amused
by the futile, breathless efforts of an aging,
overweight, and much-too-solicitous dad
to constrain a fiercely independent,
if teetering, son . . .

IV

Now it is another summer. You are twelve,
and we are on a family campout
at Johnson's Shut-ins State Park
in central Missouri. The first day we explore
the shut-ins, sunning in the shallow pools,
frolicking in the troughs and slides
formed by centuries of water cascading
over stone, or balancing like equilibrists
on the craggy rocks and tossing frisbees,
wild, darting birds, back and forth.
The second day, on your own, you discover
the diving place downriver from the shut-ins,
disregarding whether or why timid, adventureless
adults might want to deny any youngster
the exhilaration of leaping from a forty-foot
cliff into the Black River. Unnerved
but compliant, we watch you climb to the top,
walk to the edge of the cliff, pause
to measure your courage, then dare to step
into the free fall of empty space. Your small,
frail body hurtles downward, clears the rocks
at the foot of the cliff, and disappears,
*

to us interminably, in the murky water.
When you surface, to climb the rock once more,
your proud grin is as wide as our relief . . .

V

Passages all, these and others, on the way
to manhood, no less for me as for you.
Some, like the skinned arms and legs
from climbing the pinoak in the back yard
or the broken ankle from the skateboard spill,
were obvious and easily understood;
others, I now know, had to be seized,
stolen by you, and were only dimly perceived
by each of us as necessary to your sense
of freedom and self-worth. Each time
I told myself, *You must not cling, smother;*
you must remember, risk-taking is a way
of growing, and love is letting go.
But I cannot say that now.
The void you enter today is greater than any
skydive from whatever height, and far
more deadly. Forgive me, my valiant
and high-spirited son, I do not question
your courage, and I hope I do not shame you
with my faintheartedness, but I must say,
in all sincerity, I have no stomach for this war.
On this day, driving home in middle age,
as bombs and missiles and tracer bullets
flare and flame the Iraqi night
and armies hunker down for battle
in a God-forsaken desert on the far side
of the world, I long to will back
the mock-heroic words, rewind the clock,
bring you home, hold you in my arms
like the precious, newborn, innocent child
you, in that old relinquished world, once were.

On a Pier at Dana Point

Neither miles nor mind
can measure the distance
we've traveled to this reunion
with our son and his wife
on this unseasonably cold
California beach.

Nor years, though we are both
all too conscious of time
painfully, inevitably falling away
like that last visible arc
of golden sun there, far out,
over the vast Pacific.

As we stroll hand in hand,
hearts heavy as this dismal day,
our demeanors mask from strangers
the crisis that brings us together.
Yet the whole landscape seems
given over to our grief:
scattered beach fires, tiny candles,
draw the few remaining beachcombers
for comfort; three lone surfers
wearing wet suits scramble ashore,
conceding defeat.

Just ahead on the pier
our son and daughter-in-law,
young parents of the premature child
who is struggling for her life
in a hospital in another part
of this giant city, gaze into a future
as dark and mysterious as the waves
swirling underneath their feet.

All abandon logic and reason
in this cold, gray place.
The gravity of such moments
*

is reserved only for the heart.
And so we faithfully gather here,
a family drawn together by sadness,
and love, waiting not for understanding
but for some sense of recognition,
insight, feeling, which comes,
if at all, like that sudden
and hopeful surprise of silhouette
at the far end of the beach,
a lone fisherman, small and black
against the failing sky, rod lifted aloft,
casting his line into the deep,
unknown, and unknowing sea.

The Royal Touch

to Kaleigh

Today, proud grandparents
watching you being passed
from hand to hand like communion,
old and young alike,
relatives, friends, and strangers,
all eagerly awaiting their turn
to hold you in their arms
and worship at the altar
of your perfect beauty,

We recall how, short weeks ago,
we first saw you in an isolation
ward of a California hospital,
born three months premature,
weighing a pound and a half,
lying, so voiceless and still,
in a mechanical womb,
linked to breath and life
only by God's grace, your own
immeasurable will to survive,
and a frighteningly fragile system
of beeping monitors and gurgling tubes.

There, no one but your parents
and nurses could touch you, and they
only with painfully scrubbed
and rubber-gloved hands strained
through a small window in the side
of the incubator. But as they, and we,
agonized and prayed through those long,
dark days and nights of terror,
your body marvelously blossomed,
first gram by gram, then ounce by ounce,
until it matched the invisible flower
of your incredible heart's desire.

Now everyone longs to hold you,
feel the talismanic grip
of your tiny fingers, draw faith
and strength from the playful smile
of one victorious over the accidents
of misfortune and death.

Looking at this long line of worshipers,
we're reminded of how, in the old
superstitious days, people flocked
by the thousands to seek the royal touch
as cure for deformity and disease.
We still do. Miracle baby,
such a little princess you are,
but royalty nonetheless, and we,
your subjects, one by one, bring
that part of us that can still believe
and offer it for your healing touch,
hoping to fashion from your innocence
and purity a golden angel to charm away
every shadow of evil and sadness
in our misdirected and fragmented lives.

In That Winter

for Kaye

In that winter of my cold despair
we sat and watched the vagrant birds
feeding outside our kitchen window.
Daily they came in chattering herds —
woodpecker, cardinal, finch, and sparrow,
junco, thrasher, towhee, lark — all were there,
braiding their busy brightness on every limb
of the dogwood's flayed and joyless stem.

You laughed at the nervous titmouse all eye
for the hawking jay, scolded the selfish siskin race,
too jealous to share their discovered grace.

Once the stately grosbeak, stranger to our little band,
pasted its color across a blackbird's gloomy stare;
and once I found you, patient as the snow,
taming the electric chickadee with your hand.

All those days they came in ceaseless need,
and hourly you replenished their store of seed.
So too in that winter, as you know, did I —
like your friends the robin and the dove,
finding rest and hope of sunny April sky
in the windless cedars of your perfect love.

Part Three:
WORLD'S STAGE

World's Stage

"London probably has more theatres than any other city in the world."

— ***Travel Guide***

A playhouse on every corner, and everyone
you see, it appears, has gone into acting.

Like Shakespeare, that small-town youth
who discovered in the ample costumes
of Blackfriars and the Globe
those other selves to disguise the one
escaping from his father, Anne, himself.

And still today the players are all about,
and not just the professionals in the West End
or the amateurs in every church and pub:
the housewife, with her windblown hair,
fading mascara, and funereal dress,
clutching a playbill on the midnight train;
young, dreaming lovers strolling hand in hand
past the crocuses in Kensington Gardens;
yuppie businessmen, proud and self-composed,
leaning over lunch at a table in the Ritz;
the punk rocker parading with his Walkman
along the streets of Soho; a saxophonist
in a clown's face and spangled tails
playing for tips in Leicester Square;
beefeaters guarding pomp and ceremony in the Tower;
and everywhere, everywhere, the tourists —
American, Japanese, Australian, German, French —
taking one- and two-week intermissions
from God knows what sad, little lives back home.

All of London's a giant stage
where we each one come to play a part:
king or queen, lover, hero, villain, fool,
whichever role will serve to mask,
from the world and from ourselves,
the unreal characters we've become.

Underground Poem

Seated on the London Underground,
on my way to a play at a West End theatre,
I observe a young black, an African
judging by his dress, sitting alone,
his eyes fixed on the wall above
and slightly behind my head.

As unobtrusively as possible,
I follow his fixed gaze
to a framed poster displaying another
of the ubiquitous Underground Poems: this one,
Dylan Thomas's "In My Craft and Sullen Art."
I reflect on the unpredictable irony of conjunction:
a white American and an African black
coincidentally sharing the same London train
speeding through the darkness on a winter night,
unspeaking strangers, simultaneously
reading Thomas's immortal lines about time
and death, art and love.

Ah, Dylan, though you may
have scorned praise or reward
and courted indifference to your singing words,
surely you would be pleased to see your poem
commuting daily from the grave
and communing in this most public
and international of galleries
with the common heart of humanity
still questing for its destiny and dreams.

The Lovers

From my office window
I watch two lovers
lounging on the corner,
talking, laughing,
playing.

Across the distance
I enter their smiles,
siphon words
from their lips,
translate intimacy.

Distracted by duty,
I take calls, sort papers,
file reports.

When I look again
the lovers are gone.
An empty, rusting
garbage can, unnoticed before,
sprouts from the curb
like a thorn.

What Researchers Do

All alone, or with a few
like-minded groupies,
specialists in the art of pursuit,
they search through dark attics
and closets and musty archives
for that most elusive and beautiful
of all seducers, Truth,

While all about them the world
spins on, breeding desire:
teenagers in parked cars
fumbling with buttons and zippers;
lovers in mansions, houses,
cottages, apartments, tents;
adulterers between the sheets
in every motel.

Researchers all,
probing life for the hard fact
of experience that will serve,
for an hour or a day,
to give meaning to the orgastic urge
to exist.

Hospital

You can't miss it, even if you try,
there on the town's only hill
where, in the old days,
would have loomed a fortress,
or a church.

Daily we skirt its premises,
shielding our eyes to watch the ducks
shimmering on the nearby lagoon.
Like them, we would choose to float
on smooth surfaces, free
of the horror that one day we too
will cower on a fragile island
in obeisance to the inescapable
heritage of blood.

Above us, unmindful of our will,
inside those parenthetic walls
that mark our origin and destiny,
the lurking terror primes itself:
amputated stumps of arms and legs,
cancerous colons, dried fetuses,
clipped uteri, hourly consigned
to the insatiable, damnable flames.

Outside, we watch the ducks,
or gaze into the sun's bright stare
to burn from our timid minds
the knowledge of white-robed priestesses
bearing homage to the gods of death,
in processions led by approving elders
who continually wash their hands.

The River

Once the town and the adjacent river
were as inseparable as young lovers.
In those days the whole community
leaned downhill. Workers daily strolled
the cobblestone levee; youth lingered
on piers, swam; couples watched paddle-wheel
steamboats appear and disappear. All
yielded gladly to the powerful undertow
of romance and dream. Even the violent
spree of a drunken flood could scarcely
diminish the joy of cohabitation
with such a handsome, lusty god.

Now we are estranged.
The derelict husband, today our shame,
is locked behind a prison wall.
Moving westward in search of tamer, safer
loves, we seldom cast a glimpse backward,
marriage and fidelity now just vague
memories buried beneath the rising fog.
Only the bronze soldier on the courthouse
lawn remains faithful, mute sentinel unaware
that his companions have marched on.
We call it progress, this trading
of the ebb and flow of unpredictability
for the sure footing of pavement and hill.

Yet still, at night, sleeping and floating
in our placid water beds, we rouse,
half-conscious, to follow the foghorn call
of Huck and Jim, or Captain Cannon
in the pilothouse of the Robert E. Lee.

Hannibal, 1985

That authentic devil Huck
may have triumphed
in the eternal struggle
for Sam Clemens' body and soul,

but here in Hannibal,
in the heart of the country,
everything and everybody belong
to the frivolous, angelic Tom:

billboards, subdivisions,
streets, restaurants, shops,
even the restored town center
where a counterfeit Mark Twain

leans in wax on his walking stick
and gazes, with genuine civic
pride, upon the jangling parade
of tourists and strangers.

Search all you want today
among these white-washed fences
and these white-washed lives
but you'll find no trace

of that unwashed outlaw Huck,
still unregenerate and subversive,
who long ago followed his heart
downriver to the territory beyond,

or that recreant outcast Jim,
dark father, mother, savior,
for whom Huck gladly sold his soul
in futile hope of saving ours.

No, this is now Tom Sawyer's Estates,
a sleeping river town where good folks
live their safe, grammatical lives
according to the authority of the book,

and all their sons forever marry
the Becky Thatchers next door.

Church Pianist

for Marcella Sutterfield

*"I should like to speak of God not on the boundaries but at the center,
not in weakness but in strength;and therefore not in death and guilt but
in man's life and goodness."*

— *Dietrich Bonhoeffer*

Music steps from her fingers,
drawing sighs,
walks on water
above our sleeping faces
and yearning hearts.

Grocers, salesmen, clerks,
housewives, poets
lift loaves and fishes,
begging grace.

She consents,
plays on,
but, playing, remembers:

A house beside the beach,
a soldier sitting beside her,
notes of Beethoven's "Pathétique"
floating seaward,
redeeming the salty air.

Now
she plays for others,
grief rising, lifting,
through the music,
beyond the music, saying,
*This is my body, broken for you,
take and eat.*

Worshipers follow, perceiving God.

Einstein

I think of Einstein
not as the *penetralia mentis*
who squeezed the abstract
whiteness from the sun
and balanced a billion stars
upon the great, eternal
riddle of the cosmos,
splitting shibboleth
to speak a new world
into existence,

But as a young husband
and father leisurely
wheeling a baby carriage
along the streets of Berne,
measuring time and space
in the absolute distance between
a woman's relative laughter
and a child's prophetic tears.

To Richard Bach

Lines and lines
of Seagull's disciples
confirm you looked
within yourself
and found us all.

That voice you heard
we've all heard —
frail humanity's
brittle cry to soar,
unfettered,
free of earth:

The lost job,
the unpaid mortgage,
the crying child
left below,
forgotten
in that wide embrace
of cloud and wind
and sky.

Strangers to the ground,
our lives, like earth,
take on order,
harmony: tree line,
river, and plowed field
redeemed out of chaos
and fixed in timelessness.

But even this
admits limitation
you will not accept:

Man loves man
only as he may become.
To love him as he is
would require a God.

An Arrangement of a Story by Faulkner

And you on a buckskin pony
with eyes like blue electricity,
a mane like tangled fire,
galloping up the hill
into the high heaven of the world.

In Mrs. Widdrington's garret,
beneath tarred roofing paper,
the poet's skeleton resists,
desiring sleep and peace, knowing
the end of life is lying still.

But Pegasus still gallops,
wanting to perform something
bold and tragical and austere:
saying No to death.

Still galloping,
the imagination soars outward;
still galloping,
it thunders up
the long blue hill of heaven,
its tossing mane
in golden swirls like fire,
a dying star upon the immensity
of blackness and of silence.

But from the thunder, punily
diminishing, reincarnated,
rises the poet's voice:
The flesh is dead, living on itself,
consuming itself in its own renewal;
but I will never die,
for I am the Resurrection
and the Life,
saying No to death,
again and again and again.

Epilogue

The revels have ended.
Prospero exits,
melting into art's thin eternity.
The dream is rounded.

Yet something remains:
haunting vision
of utopia less remote,
tenacious hope
that tragedy is comedy,
sentiment for even
the Calibans of the world.

The audience departs.

Sunlight glistens on Moor Ditch.
England is England still,
but Prospero's island, too.

The play is over.
Now the play begins.

.

Part Four:
DARKNESS RISES

Darkness Rises

Darkness does not fall.
Darkness rises
from the ground up.

Stand in the lowest valley
and watch the night
engulf the tallest hill.

First the grass,
then the trees,
then the hills and mountains,
and only then the sky.

Darkness rises,
covering all.

But that, too, is deceit,
another concealment of nature
to test the soul.

Actually, it is light,
that eternal vampire sun,
which sucks, ounce by ounce
and juice by juice,
its own sustenance
from the resplendent earth.

Denying that, the whole universe
becomes one immense black hole,
lightless, bottomless, anonymous,
absurd.

Like man, that epiphany,
when robbed of that slight
sliver of sundown
just beyond the farthest hill.

Spring Warfare

On this spring morning
the field behind our house
decodes messages of battle.

Artilleries of rain pound
the heart-shaped leaves
of the redbud tree.

Bluejays strafe bivouacking
wrens and cardinals,
while battalions of blackbirds
plunder defenseless villages
of insects and worms.

A robin's small arms chatter
warns comrades of approaching
panzer cats.

Soon summer's truce
will relinquish the dead,
turn survivors to songs
of forgetfulness and joy.

But next winter, as last,
a one-legged titmouse will cling
to the feeder beside our window,
claiming veterans' benefits.

One Looks at Two

In an open pasture,
halting my foot in midstride,
I narrowly avoid crushing
two mating butterflies.

Leering down,
a connoisseur of voyeurs,
I examine their gold-pulsing
embrace, as unabashed
in their public nakedness
as a pair of Woodstock lovers.

Then, prurience satisfied,
I wonder if it is the weight,
or ecstasy, of coupling
that makes these ethereal darlings
condescend to earth, oblivious
even to the shadow of annihilation
lodged above their quivering forms.

As if in reply, they lift off,
genitalia still fused, hover
briefly to reclaim their element,
then speed toward the neighboring woods.

I follow, as best I can,
through weeds, past terraces,
curious to trace in any sphere
a marriage of such union,
tenacity, endearment.

Later, abandoning the field
for an asphalt road leading home,
I recall that Ruskin, that bitter
prophet, warned against the fallacy
of equating nature with the unhinged
desires of our own making. Perhaps
he too had chased the fluttering
fidelity of butterflies.

The Circling Hawk Descends

for Jim Hamby

The circling hawk
descends,
familiar as breath
on this late autumn air.
The year subsides
in fragments of song.

Spectator now,
you walk a dry, brown field
to find in trees
mementos of color,
miniscule delights.
A goldfinch flashes,
freezes,
awaiting benediction.

On the sidelines of consciousness
Saturday's heroes revive
beneath Kant's leaning steeples.
Little brothers and sisters,
body pales, and intellect,
but essences endure,
live on,
comfort the air, the ear,
like the nightingale's song:
Venite a laudare
per amore cantare . . .

In this still meadow
lenses narrow a spinning landscape
to the sparrow's beady eye,
canvas enough to sketch
sacraments of praise
on the abstract riddle
of the world.

First Snowfall

Entranced, I watch from my study window
as branches of youthful trees,
unaccustomed to such grave design,
accept the keen embrace of early snow
without reply. Sluggish as the breeze,
birds bury their songs in pantomime.
A slow-motion landscape robbed of sound,
the scene portends a universe winding down.

Frightened by the terror in so much stillness,
I rush outdoors, inhale the loud caress
of icy cold, delight as the sleety snow
xylophones through the remnant leaves.
Attuned to my unhoused, reborn ear,
water dripping steadily from the eaves
bids answer to the time of year
with ceaseless cymbals and ecstasies.

At the St. Louis Arch

There
the rush of traffic
rattles
the city's
anxious day.

And there
the betraying river
hurries
icefloes
to southern meltings.

But here
a rainbow curve
of silver steel
cancels a leaden
winter sky,

And, beckoned,
we ascend
to saner measure,
slower sound.

New Year: January 1992

Throughout the night
the unexpected snow fell, like grace,
upon the wounded and mangled lives
in every house and street,
bandaging the limbs of every tree
and shrub, silently covering
discarded Christmas trees
awaiting curbside pickup on Price Drive,
wrecked cars rusting out
in Johannes' salvage yard on Kingshighway,
trash and litter swirling about
the parking lot of West Park Mall,
used condoms in Cherokee Park.

Next morning the earliest risers,
commuters to Proctor and Gamble
north of town and morning shift workers
at Florsheim Shoe, pause in their doorway
or drive, reluctant to be the first
to scatter footprints on the conscience
of the pristine and moon-blanched beauty
of the fresh-painted ground.

Some Leaves Go Down to Winter

Some leaves go down to winter's call
at the slightest coaxing of an autumn breeze,
eagerly forfeiting their grace of green
in speckled frolic beyond the taunt of trees.

Some leaves go down to winter's squall
in raging defiance at the screaming blow,
hurling a brown and withered dream
against the sweep of vast, enveloping snow.

But from my window I relish sight
of leaves on pinoaks lingering still
beyond the fondling of an autumn's will,
beyond the buffeting of a winter's night,
to be gently nudged at last to earth
by budding springtime's rising, bursting birth.

A Single Flower

for Kaye, Laurie, and Stephen

That was the year some said
spring would never come.
Close-fisted April held Easter
hostage under threat of snow.
The persecution of sun seemed endless.

Even the dogwood which is first
to blossom acquiesced to days of gloom.
Or so we thought — until we chanced
to glimpse a single flower, one
splendid inflorescence, impatient
with nature's delay, breaking winter's
strangling hold to possess the air.
Except for this one unaccountable utterance,
the whole tree spoke not a single word.

We called the children to witness
the anomaly. Together, fascinated
and strangely renewed, we watched
the eager pinkness warm the sun,
loose the frozen gears of the season,
peel the silence from the tight-throated days.

In Praise of New Beginnings

I set this down
in praise
of new beginnings:

the winding of a clock,
runners awaiting
the starter's gun,
all inaugurations,
commencements, grand openings,
ordinations, christenings,
weddings,
every madonna with child,
middle-aged losers
strolling hand in hand,
a robin feeding her young,
a new moon, a new year,
another decade.

Raise the curtain!
Cut the ribbon!
Lift the glass!

What celestial
symphonies of faith:
the heavy downbeat of history
drowned in ringing hosannas
of hope.

Perpendicular Rain

If, my children,
you must know grief,
pray let it descend
as perpendicular rain,
somewhere far beyond
the ravenous edge
of slashing wind
and thunderous regret
and gently, delicately
held in balance
with soft siftings
of radiant sun.

Look, here,
beneath the passing cloud,
on the dogwood's
once-bitter leaves,
where tears, transfigured,
now trace
innumerable threads
of silver hope.

Picking Strawberries

You learn, after a while,
that the best ones always
lie close to the ground,
finding their red lushness
among leaves, pine needles,
rotting newsprint.

It seems not merely
the weight of gravity,
but some nameless and happy
compulsion to identify
with earth, to blend every ripeness
with the source that engenders it.

Thin, sterile stems lift
green berries toward the sky,
while all fruition leans earthward,
even God's, we are told.

Robert Hamblin was born in Jericho, Mississippi, in 1938. He holds undergraduate degrees from Northeast Mississippi Community College and Delta State University and an M.A. and Ph.D. from the University of Mississippi. He is Professor of English as well as Director of the Center for Faulkner Studies at Southeast Missouri State University in Cape Girardeau. Mr. Hamblin also serves as associate editor of *The Cape Rock* and as poetry editor for *Aethlon: The Journal of Sport Literature*. His first book of poems, *Perpendicular Rain*, appeared in 1986.

Also available from **Time Being Books**

LOUIS DANIEL BRODSKY
You Can't Go Back, Exactly
The Thorough Earth
Four and Twenty Blackbirds Soaring
Mississippi Vistas: Volume One of *A Mississippi Trilogy*
Forever, for Now: Poems for a Later Love
Mistress Mississippi: Volume Three of *A Mississippi Trilogy*
A Gleam in the Eye: Poems for a First Baby
Gestapo Crows: Holocaust Poems

WILLIAM HEYEN
Erika: Poems of the Holocaust
Pterodactyl Rose: Poems of Ecology
Ribbons: The Gulf War — A Poem

LOUIS DANIEL BRODSKY and **WILLIAM HEYEN**
Falling from Heaven: Holocaust Poems of a Jew and a Gentile

RODGER KAMENETZ
The Missing Jew: New and Selected Poems

Please call or write for a free catalog.

TIME BEING BOOKS
POETRY IN SIGHT AND SOUND

Saint Louis, Missouri

10411 Clayton Road • Suites 201-203
St. Louis, Missouri 63131
(314) 432-1771

TO ORDER TOLL-FREE
(800) 331-6605 Monday through Friday, 8 a.m. to 4 p.m. Central time
FAX: (314) 432-7939